Wading through Lethe

Paulette Guerin

FUTURECYCLE PRESS
www.futurecycle.org

Cover photo by Noah Darnell; author photo by Noah Darnell; cover and interior design by Diane Kistner; Adobe Garamond Pro text and titling

Library of Congress Control Number: 2021949650

Published by FutureCycle Press
Athens, Georgia, USA

ISBN 978-1-952593-20-8

For my grandmothers,
Katherine Black and Jackie Guerin

Contents

III

I

Ginkgo

Through rain-thrash
and wind-sear,
the stems cling
to each limb.

After other trees
have metamorphosed
green to gold,
red to brown,
stems rattle in the dawn.

The ginkgo waits,
then lets go.
Brief burst
of yellow.

First Communion

The night before, Grandma made my pallet
on the couch with faded blue flowers.

Across the room, the iron-barrel stove loomed.
We learned not to touch it.

At midnight I woke. I'd never heard rain on a tin roof
and was sure what Revelation promised was true—

dark horses had come. In church we'd learned
about the wise and foolish virgins with their oil.

I had not confessed my sins. Everyone else slept—
or were they gone? Then the rain let up.

The dark turned dim. I chipped the polish
from my nails, ashamed they were not bare.

Emergence

The summer our parents split, we spent our days
at St. Mary's. June's heat had drawn the water
from the ground. As the sun incubated the air,
cicadas crawled from their burrows and screeched

into being. Males called out with ribbed
bellies; females rubbed their wings in answer,
flitting on stone statues of saints, squirming
in the crevices of robes or folded hands.

The windows vibrated with mating calls,
sparse rugs barely absorbing the sound.
Icons looked down from plaster walls,
their eyes distant like someone lost or in love.

Dishwashing

After lunch, the nuns took volunteers
to help wash the dishes. They loaded

the racks while I dried, clean cups and plates
hot enough to burn. They worked in silence,

desires concealed like a tree's rings.
I enjoyed not having to speak,

attended by childless mothers.

Roots

The condos stood like dominoes.
Without a line for sky and land to meet,
even sunny days had long shadows.
Mother's tulips went missing,
and then our home looked like every other,
the same sad squares for windows.

One day we left. I learned the way sunlight
can fill a field of hay and rain pound
a tin roof through the night.
Amid baying coyotes and bullfrog moans, I found
a pink dogwood deep in the shadowed canopy,
its rare color drawn from the ground.

Milking

The women slipped her head
between the fork of a tree.
I braced a board against the bark,

a makeshift stock. Mrs. Henry kept the rope
taut around the legs while Grandma
milked the bleating nanny.

The swollen bag shrank.
The runty kid approached slowly,
still afraid of hooves.

Smoothing out her wrinkled dress,
Mrs. Henry said her grandbaby
would be visiting soon.

Then softly, "But she's got
no fingers on one hand.
Umbilical cord, you know."

Grandma frowned, then said, "Still you're lucky,"
placing her hand above her heart
just below the neck.

Summer of '95

We sold blueberries in front of the hardware store.
It was hard for us not to eat them. All day

the smell of rubber, wood, and sweet tobacco wafted out
with the swinging door, its ringing bell.

It had been a summer of hot sunrises,
the day's embers smoldering into night.

It sucked the plants dry like a smoker taking a drag.
There'd be no more mornings when we ate our fill.

We made eighteen dollars that day.
Mother didn't say if that was much,

or enough, or if she was glad
that what we didn't sell was entirely ours.

Mountain Air

Mornings, air filtered through window screens,
heavy with moisture

that waked the grass. In winter,
the air was thin; in drought, alive

with dust and pine. The smell descending
with dusk told us the time,

that our minutes were being swallowed
into the blue glow along the horizon,

where, in summer, we stayed under the stars,
sky blacker than coffee or tar.

At the Creek

"If only my memory were sharp again," she said,
sitting on a stump near the creek's edge.

I waded in the shallow cool, pants rolled, wet.
Her straw hat brimmed a shadow

over her face. The stones shimmered, each more
dazzling than the last.

I pulled out one to show her,
but it lost its luster when it left the water.

Chicken Farm

The squawks and flaps
are like a host of angels falling.

Feathers scatter with each step,
a swirl of snow flurries.

Her family uses the remains—
feet fried, eyes pickled.

On the bank of the river,
a steering wheel dangles

from a rope. While the boys
swing and jump, she skips stones,

noting the brief buoyancy
before each is sucked back into the river.

Daffodil

The idea of green

beaks out
of a motherless egg,

its shovel tongue
thrusting

in the winter's dark.

Rapunzel

She combs her hair with a pig-bristle brush,
the window's light casting a yellow square

into the darkened grass. She wishes the girl
in the glass were older, fairer, and in love,

then she looks beyond, into the shapeless night,
her eyes lit with wanderlust at the late call

of the whippoorwill. Ribbons of hair
collect at her feet just as dew falls from the air.

She dreams of a dance, another's hands on her waist,
then leans out to measure how far the locks will reach.

Churchgoing

Red dust covered the cars,
wheels digging ruts in the dirt road
twice on Sundays and once mid-week.

While our parents prepped for Sunday's soul-saving,
we walked the roads that wound into the woods
around the country church.

Imagining the heat of another's mouth,
we verged toward sinful ways
in thought, if not deed.

Though we squirmed in pews the next day,
on Saturdays the threat of being damned
seemed a reasonable price to pay.

Y2K

I turned fifteen and waited for a beginning,
then an end. Mother stocked the cabinets with cans.
In the safe, she kept paper slips

with our names, dates, ink footprints.
On New Year's Eve, Grandma brought over
the gun she kept beneath her pillow.

We ate our lucky black-eyed peas
and watched the ball drop. The radio sat in the corner,
batteries splayed around it like empty shells.

Ghost Town

Another tie chipped into the river, hitting sky.
The boys stripped their shirts, hooking them
on iron spikes in the rotten wood of the train bridge.

The scent of rain clung to the underside
of every leaf; silkworms pillowed
poison sumacs along the bank.

The boy I liked jumped first.
He sank into the deadly green, then rose
like something Hell had sent back.

I didn't jump, just straddled
a beam, wishing for a train.

In summer, the church doors opened early.
We dragged our feet through sweaty grass.
I played piano, banging weak keys.

The strings had tired of song
or preferred the boarded-up saloons
once lighting the railway line.

What can wash away my sin?
*Nothing but the blood
of Jesus.*

The ceiling fan purred over the cicada hum,
over another century's iron spikes and wood.

Summer, Greers Ferry Lake

Like graduating seniors, the cicadas emerged
after seventeen years in the ground,
starved and full of lust. I waited
for one boy's annual return,
on vacation at our lake cupped in the Ozarks.
The trees hadn't been fully painted in,
needing a hard rain and a few hot days
to brush the landscape fat and green.

The dry creek bed moved with mating,
their song swarming us to silence. At the end
of August, the sun resigned, the water turned cold.
I woke from our dream. Shells littered
the ground like candy wrappers,
then vanished beneath the leaves.

Morrilton, Arkansas

Train cars jump in and out
of old storefront windows.

A boy in Levi's crosses the tracks
toward the monument company's headstones.

A few already have a chiseled name.
I wait for him behind a heap of brick

and corrugated tin. On windy days,
the paper-mill stink drifts into town.

He claims the money beats baling hay,
then closes his mouth over mine.

Moth

She lay edged in the door's crevice,
brown wings splayed against the white.

Deep in folded wool or powdery flour,
there's a borrowed bed, a stolen hour.

Grandmother

You know the details of your wedding day,
but aren't sure if you planted beans or peas.
You can't remember what you did today.

You boil the eggs 'til water burns away,
but make for lunch homemade pimento cheese.
Tell me again about your wedding day

as if the meal you shared were yesterday.
I ask you where you might have lost your keys;
you can't remember what we did today.

Something is wrong. I don't know what to say.
I'm still amazed that you recall with ease
the names of guests who shared your wedding day,

the baby's breath tucked into your bouquet.
You teach me how to paint the fallen leaves,
but can't remember what we did today.

When he comes home, he asks about your day.
You say you'd rather hear about his. Please!
You know the details of your wedding day,
but can't remember what you did today.

A week before she died,

I ate one of her lemon bars,
thinking nothing of holding
something so delicate
it lost its shape in my hand.

Funeral Wreath

A gaudy bouquet drapes the coffin
like a tired spider, and twisted around wire hearts,
the little pink rosettes you'd expect.
Off to the side, a blue-ribboned wreath
wears shrunken leaves bent around hard stalks
blooming cotton bolls—unspun, undyed,
unwoven. Though forty years a schoolteacher,
her early life was like most others'
in post-Depression Arkansas: nimble fingers
slipping loose the cotton, at first soft,
then dry, then sharp, the fangs of the stalk
ready to strike. Nearly a century earlier,
she worked, sun on neck, something like a song
on her tongue, fingers bleeding, the sack of cotton light.

Diminuendo

We left the upright, one side propped
with *As I Lay Dying,* decaled roses peeling,
the black varnish buckled after years
of playing *Sonata No. 8 in C Minor.* A train rolled by,
the strings humming in its wake.

We packed the row of photographs
above the chipped ivories. I picked up
Mother's cricket cage, the only thing
for which she'd ever paid full price.

Yellow leaves shimmied to the ground. A new moon
kept the sky dark, the stars too weak.
I almost left the key in the bird feeder tray.

II

Hurricane Party, East Laville Hall

School's a month in. They're still on Homer,
but headed for the tragedies. TV says Gustav has made landfall.
Soon the Baton Rouge sky will be thick
as roux. Mouton gulps

her fifth instant cappuccino. She hasn't brushed
her teeth in weeks. Thibodaux heads to the hall bath
before the dorm loses power. In less than five minutes,
she's ankle-deep in runoff.

She shaves in case this is the big one. Casanova knocks
on room 102. He's brought a gallon, he says with a wink,
of sweet tea. Mouton leaves. Halfway down the hall, Thibi gags
on what smells like fried onion, blooming.

It's Mouton's love of burnt popcorn.
Thibi opens the window, and a humid wind
licks pages. A strange guy she's seen a couple times
is on the roof, cloud-gazing in the rain. A TV report

from New Orleans shows the billboard
of an injury lawyer take flight, then cuts to waves swirling
like shark fins. The guy leans into the room, dripping wet,
asking if she'd like coffee at Vieux Carré.

She thinks of Penelope weaving the shroud,
nightly unraveling her youth for a man
who'll want to leave the moment he's home.
The storm comes. She goes.

Boys over Flowers, a K-drama

A kimchi-eating pauper is whisked away
to a high school of plutocrats.

"She's so lucky! She must have saved lives
in her previous lives." It's what outsiders

like to say. *My goal in life is to gain things
with my ability,* says the modern-day Pip.

Each episode, a new problem;
boy tries to fix problem; she finds her own way.

Usually, she just works harder, longer.
She says, *the person who lit the fire*

should put it out. Of course, she has options—
the richest boy in South Korea or his best friend.

For me, the story should end
there: what does love matter

so long as there's meat? Then Little Brother utters:
Pride is more important than money,

and I remember my mother refusing
suitor after suitor, seeing through

their spit-shined armor, knitting a life
and waiting for no man's return.

An Education

On TV when woman meets man
to try him out she asks him
to come up for a drink. That's code
for *you can have sex with me,*
not *I really want to show you my African violet—*
did you know that you can't touch the leaves
without hurting it? The man is polite and takes the drink,
acts amused by the décor, feigns interest
in the fragile African violet.
So if I ask someone up,
even if it is just to meet my cat,
he will think I'm sending a signal:
my body is yours. I will think, maybe
I'm supposed to send this signal, am supposed
to like another's footfall on the stairs,
his hand on the small of my back
as if to guide me, as if I don't know where I'm going,
as if I have to know where I'm going.

Airport

A woman looks at us from her wheelchair,
speaking a language no one understands.
Behind her, planes glide by as if empty,

and I wonder when I last did anything
for its own sake. A blue knob of sky
turns gray. Over the intercom, a voice

offers money to anyone willing to wait.
Where we land, smoke screens
the mountains; the sun blisters.

I enter a sepia world the color of things past
and wonder if glancing back would mean the end
of faith, the loss of promised things.

Cloudburst

We lose an hour halfway
through Georgia. Rain taps the hood.

I pull away from the cloud line,
a few beats ahead of the melody,

then exit east, storm in rear view.
Afraid to stop,

I cut through town after town,
name after forgotten name.

Pleasant Street

Lined with hundred-year-old houses
in Cape Cod blue or Harlequin green,

fences straight as teeth,
the street lies shadowed by trees

wearing stoles of Spanish moss. Daily rain
brushes them clean, leaving debris

matted like carrion. Next door
a voice lectures from behind her porch screen.

She has so much left to say. Hospice takes care
of the laundry. On the corner,

a bent woman tends purple flowers
shaped like gramophones.

Feral cats drowse on her lawn.
In the warming air, clover conspires a takeover.

A reddish grasshopper chews mimosa cud;
he's as long and hungry as a clothespin.

Santa Maria Maggiore, Ferentino, Italy

"Fiat lux," the priest says, slipping into the Latin
of his youth. The stones of the Gothic church
all but demand it.

The words bounce off cross vaults and apse
in a pidgin of human and divine,
unexpressed as Michelangelo's *Slaves*.

Sunlight washes the round window,
shadows tottering on its stone ledge—mostly crows,
here and there a flit of sparrow. Lest we forget,

Christ hangs on a cross strung between clustered columns
too thick to put one's arms around.
They're like the grove

on the school playground
where we played tag, the hollow oak, home base.
Lightning struck the tree one spring;

seven children died.
In the communion line, my hands in prayer
open. I wish the nave were more

than a capsized ship. In Hell, Sisyphus forgets
his punishment, yells
to no one as the stone rolls away.

Still Life

after Caravaggio

Light freckles the fruit basket.
The pear has reached its peak,
a nipple waiting for a mouth.
A persimmon clings to the spine
of a broken stem. Along the woven rim,
black grapes are crushed
in shadow. Fig leaves curl into scythes
and dangle as if from tiny gallows.
An apple worm inches on
in search of a different heaven.

Leaving Rome

Along the Spanish Steps, streetlights popped on
like syncopated fireflies. Walking up Via del Corso,
I passed shop mannequins with averted eyes,
pulled my coat tighter, thinking of Keats,
dead at twenty-five. A cyclone of cars spun
at the foot of Vittorio Emanuele's grimy shrine.
The Colosseum's pocked crown rose above
the Forum's broken bones. I mailed a postcard,
the scene depopulated and clean, knowing
it would arrive months before I returned home,
knowing it looked nothing like what I'd seen.

The Ecstasy of St. Teresa

The seraph holds the arrow. He's not
a dimpled cherub Raphael might paint.
The Bernini stands, a boy turned man, his wing
outstretched. Between the thumb and finger
of the other hand he rubs her gown, as thin
as gauze but more alive than anything
he's ever touched. She does not watch him raise
the fiery tip, avoiding his gaze. Curved lips
go slack, her lidded eyes half close. No matter
that death's a one-time lover who will take
her maidenhead and run. Maybe she'll live,
describe the angle of the burn, the sear
of arrow ripping heart from chest, the pain
so sweet she would not pray for a reprieve.

Monument to Dante

Florence has finally decided to find room for him
among other greats interred in Santa Croce—
Galileo, Machiavelli, Michelangelo—

figuring, *if we build it, they will come,*
and we do, we always have,
but Ravenna won't give him up.

Once before, friars walled up the bones,
afraid that during night's dead hour
a Florentine band of priests would exhume him

in the name of Beatrice, in whose honor
the deed could never be a sin.
Now street signs bespeak his *Commedia,*

restaurants promise a taste of paradise.
Merchants offer red-robed reproductions
on the face of a million postcards

for would-be poets on pilgrimage—
no place hallowed, no place free
from quills and ink wells, wax and seals.

Musée d'Orsay

Not water lilies floating behind plexiglass
or the icy stare
of van Gogh's self-portrait,
but the ballerinas
buoyant yet balanced *en pointe*
compelled the man's cry.

All heads turned toward him, strapped
in his wheelchair.
He could not tell the nurse
to let him linger
at Degas's frozen figures.

The rest of us resumed our reverie,
waiting to be moved.

At the Jardin des Plantes

Zoo-goers walk blindly past a white owl
sitting meekly, his cage too small

for flight. Across the walkway, teal peacocks
shriek as passersby tease them for their tails.

In spite of beaks poised to attack
and sounds a far cry from a siren's call,

they are too beautiful not to stare; so we look,
even as the feathered fan sees all.

Windy City, 54th Floor

Tired of being marooned,
our piano lost its tune,

its song like a forgotten address
among city blocks, a cold caress.

My eyes meet the moon's knowing glare.
I feed my ex-lover's orphaned plants beer,

knowing he won't come back to correct
my carelessness. Tonight the memories infect

small lamplight with a shadowed epitaph.
On the ledge, I toss our last photograph.

He packed his Beatles, Stones, The Cure,
the years an expensive souvenir.

Composition 912

Rothko painted the line
where land and sky backed into each other.
Sometimes the surface flaked
to show what lay beneath.
Sometimes the heart bled through.

Always a War

The taxi driver pointed past the roadblocks
and the protesters who had flooded
the muddy plaza. I tipped him two euro

and dragged a suitcase down the cobblestones.
Behind me voices cried against some injustice
or some war. I had come to see *Guernica,*

not baton-wielding police, a festering crowd,
a saturated sky. I'd wanted a place hot enough
to dry out a wound. The hotel was still,

the room too empty. I left.
A flamenco guitar echoed
through the subway's coves, and I glanced back

for my lover not there. The rain washed me
beneath the city. *Love brandishes
her sharpest blade,* so the song said.

Inishmore

Passengers navigate the ferry's plank
as gray waves roll over in the wind.

Gulls police the space between sea and sky,
always beneath the rain. The tourists

drift indoors for trad and a pint.
Breaking ranks, she stays by the bank.

It's her first trip; but the stones,
landscape greens, and thin clouds

are eerily familiar, like a forgotten letter
in her own handwriting

or a snapshot of herself
she can't remember being taken.

After Brueghel's Landscape with the Fall of Icarus

It's anybody's story—
sipping martinis on the cruise ship,
throwing the olives overboard.

The deck smells of baking coconut
and lawn-chair plastic. Hairy men
lounge in Speedos, nothing like the brochure.
While I ponder if the dueling pianos

will play Billy Joel again tonight, a bird—
no, a fish—splashes a colossal cannonball
in the distance. No one else notices, or cares,
and who knows if it really happened at all?

The Little Mermaid Vacations in Florida

They avoid the main drag of seafood shacks
with happy crustaceans on their signs.
She no longer collects human things.
She wants sand dollars, sea anemone.
It's been too long since she's slipped
into the water's second skin. At night,

she doesn't doubt her legs around him
as his hands find the small of her back.
Each morning she rubs her knees,
stares at painted toes. Sometimes she forgets
how to walk, spending hours in the bath.
If youth is possibility, adulthood is choice.

Now she swims until the water is cold,
no longer hearing him on his cell.
There's just the water-whipped
rush of some large fish snagging a meal.
She's heard of people who swim
so far they can't go back.

Epiphany

She sits at the bar, sucking on a cocktail clogged
with too much fruit. Broken umbrella.
God's message in the toilet stall—
"Call any time you're lonely."
Is that a 5 or an 8 in the flecking paint?

The chapel's waxy votives make her sweat.
She wants to ask why St. Sebastian
is still riddled with arrows,
but the chinking censer clogs her throat.

All around lie men famous for their wounds,
their martyrdoms, marble tombs.
The women are mostly worshipped for their wombs.

A Monastery in Venice

I woke, feet drawn
into fetal curl,
the thrum of bells
calling for prayer.

The umbrella of his hand
rested on my hip,
the gap between
our beds too wide.

In the morning air,
birds darted as if
they'd just learned flight.

Above our heads,
Christ's heart beamed,
the other walls bare.

The Eternal City

I.

White hair wisping from a silk scarf,
she takes our clothes to wash.
We've spent our daily ration,
return to the convent-turned-hostel.
Under the Virgin's gaze,
we lift the iron beds
to keep their legs from scraping the marble.

I shutter the window, the nuns below
in a beaded hour of prayer.
We slip off layers.
How much is safe to excavate?
Another woman's name is written
on his body, artifact of a buried world.

In Venice, we had masks, the spirit
of Carnival, a lagoon of refracted light
to pitch our wishes in
while we coursed an island of petrified pine
among Byzantine faces
of carefully-placed broken pieces.

In Rome the sky
is further,
the past deeper,
as we teeter along excavation pits,
enamored of dusty marble,
someone else's fragments.

In the Jewish quarter
he buys me candied fruit.
We sit in the non-breeze,
and when we get up
his shoe soles stick,
strings of melted rubber
yawning from the pavement.
Thinned by the heat,
we lose our words.

Seeking darkness, we cross the threshold
of one of Rome's 400 churches.
Our eyes go blind.
We sit beneath arches of stone,
all around us, Baroque ornaments
to draw God's gaze
or elevate our own.

II.

Pentecost at the Pantheon: small flames
flank the tombs of artists, kings.
Sunlight drips from the eye, sky punctuated there.
Constantine consecrated this ground
but the name remains: a temple for all gods.
We ask to stay for Mass. They unclasp
the ropes; we step into the circle
of light, catching snatches of the service.
Then silence. One hundred thousand poppy petals
float down, red in sun, black in shadow,
recalling tongues of fire. We do not partake
of the wine changed to blood, only watch
the petals flow as if from a wound.

III.

We have enough change
to share a gelato, the only cold thing

in the city. I choose grapefruit.
His smile turns bitter.

I think: I can swallow his pain.
Except I look back at what's left

of Rome's ruins,
where incorrigible marble

erodes beneath a grain of sand,
a drop of water.

IV.

I take him to see *The School of Athens,*
the Sistine Chapel.

I've been before, amid crowds, but today's trip
is a first: with him, my hand

in the cup of his hand. The room dampens
with body heat. How much does our breath destroy?

No one cares for the Vatican's modern religious art.
We peer into each room as if we've stumbled

upon a monk praying in his cell.
We wait in line for *The Last Judgment.*

Faces are peeled off like clothes, bodies shaken out
like old rugs, Michelangelo's enemies

immortalized there. I lift my chin like a heron
swallowing a snake

to glimpse the almost-touching fingertips.
We're ushered out in babbling languages,

sucked forward like Orpheus
to light, heat, persistent hunger.

V.

The cross-breeze raises a cobweb
like a ghost. It settles into a gauzy hammock.
The nuns are praying the rosary,

their voices climbing to our window
with afternoon shadows.

Santa Maria, Madre di Dio, prega per noi peccatori,
adesso e nell'ora della nostra morte. Amen.

It is the hour of our death,
of tossing a coin over my shoulder

without looking. The summer fever breaks.
The millions of us above ground

hurry on to evening comforts.
A beggar on his knees since morning

picks up his mat and stumbles
home, pockets bulging with *spicci,*

change. I think about *spezie,* spices, once used
as currency. Are we after flavor or money?

Out slips that word: *love.*
The black sky lies

prostrate over the city's light.
Castel Sant'Angelo rises like Mount Purgatory.

The Holy Door is closed, bolted.
Our sins will have to wait to be forgiven.

VI.

Ristorante Gli Angeli—
In girum imus nocte et consumimur igni.

Night shows up looking for recruits,
briefcase and forms to sign.

We're willing
to scrawl our names

to anything
so long as it's irrevocable.

Our glasses touch and chink,
a frail sound.

You offer the last bite of tiramisu.
I said leave it,

imagine it there waiting for us,
imagine us still there.

III

You can never go home again

but if you do,

driving beneath cocooned orbs
of interstate lights,

exiting toward a darkness
where deer emerge like memories

you hope to swerve and miss,
resist

thinking you could be anything
beyond what this place expects,

that you won't open your mouth
for the bit.

Flight

Bone-white crosses still marked Burnt Ridge
where some teen went over the edge.
The Baptist preachers proclaimed it
part of God's plan. I'd come back

for the reunion, only to find things missing:
the shaved-ice stand, out-of-state plates headed
for the lake, the boy I'd loved who bussed tables
at Bogie's. The golf course had yellowed;

the Racquet Club had burned to the ground,
the floor where we'd danced at prom a slab of ash.
Down by the water, On the Fly was locked,
the carp the only mouths that greeted me.

Though I'd never sneaked to the lake
to get wasted, he and I dove off the cliffs
one April, naked, then watched a deer
swim to Sugarloaf.

I spent that summer promising him
I would visit. Like Orpheus, when I dared
look back, I saw only clouds of dust
and no chance for mercy.

Home

I carry a basket of wet clothes,
the weight like a grudge I refuse to toss out.

The shirts hang limply, sleeves splayed.
A forest-green dress

has been bleached a shade of grass;
blood-red shirts fade to rust.

Once dry, light pierces them.
I slip into the stiffened skins.

Mercy

An early morning storm closes
around us like a fist, shallow light
wrung out in little pools.

Mold smudges darken on the tenements;
trees along the fence-line
twinge black. Wearing his overalls,

Grandpa would have said, *It's tornado weather,*
but the air isn't yet the color
of a nearly-healed bruise—green

with yellow glow. It's only water
clouding the distance, no heaven-earth
entanglements. A simple fall.

Cleaning Out the Attic

I lift her from a bed of musty clothes
ribboned with mold, the porcelain doll Grandma
gave me when I was a girl.

She's heavy as a newborn and just as breakable.
Her face is dirty. I feel like a bad mother.

I bathe her with a damp cloth,
careful at the tiny fingers
reaching out, the lips open slightly in mid-cry

or coo. I use Q-tips to clean the eyelids,
supporting her head in my palm.

Were Grandma alive, she'd say
It's not too late, and I'd pretend not to understand
the wish for something whole, unbroken.

Childhood

I'm still waiting for the mail-in rebate.
I'd like to have my money back, to spend it again;
but those bills aren't printed anymore.
The new ones don't buy as much. And what is there
to buy but unhappiness, in contrast to all there was before—
except perhaps a lampshade for the bald lightbulb?

If every step is a misstep, where's Virgil
to tell me what the twisted tail means?
I've lost currency and am taken with the current,
wading through Lethe. I'd like another season
of gold-green, an extra helping of nostalgia, please,
to press myself into a familiar mold;
instead I walk these grease-shined streets
as a foreigner, not as a prodigal come home.

Life Insurance

My email dings like a microwave.
The papers have arrived.
I'm old enough to know that the wind ripping the leaves
from a row of birches outside my window
is neither theophany nor a fresh metaphor,
not even if the leaves were a young girl's
tangled hair, the wind her grandmother's rough hand
dragging a brush hard enough to account for all
the child's imperfections. *Keep your legs together;*
you're a lady. A company has quantified my worth,
a staggering amount, which must mean
the leaves will worm out of branches next spring.

Photograph

My memory of him sits
at the bottom of an empty bottle.
When I find his picture
tucked in a book from that summer,
the bottle becomes full,
and even water has the flavor of wine.

I wonder what his face looks like now,
where lines have formed, why.
I'm past wondering what would have been
or who he's become, giving myself permission
to think of us as simply in love, once.

In my old dreams, I watched him
look for me. Now I search behind each face
for his, for one that has the memory
when we thought we had it all, and did.

Art's Folly

I visit the places we used to go.
The artwork has changed, the seats
are just as hard, the coffee too hot.
The paintings show a beach outing,
acrylic probably. He'd know. It's a tease,
the gentle lavishment of light on waves,
pale bodies leaping unscathed.
None of the paintings show what comes after:
driving home, sand reeking of washed-up crabs
and other dead, the unlit house
where no one waits. Nor the ashes
of burnt skin in the bed
or the phoenix rising, raw and tender,
unprepared for birth.

At the Coffee Shop

I saw myself in twenty years,
feet in flats, together. I've lost
another parent, rivers of grief
are crosshatched with crow's feet—
I make myself smile as I order.
I've given up on giving up
coffee. I've learned the way
my body moves through space,
how far the ceiling floats above,
how to touch what lies beneath.

I saw myself twenty years ago,
licking a finger to turn a page,
unaware of the line, my mother
holding my baby brother, her order:
a double espresso, an apple juice.
I have nothing to give up
but fear of the ghost
patrolling the hall. I'd give up the night,
but it's a given in this strange world
populated with imaginary friends,

where the self is not one but many.

Cyclist with Two Bikes

A woman pedals while holding
the handlebars of another bike.

It's as if a ghost rides carefully beside her.
They are too close to make balance easy,

and I remember after her death
wanting to feel that closeness, however precarious,

while bagging embroidered handkerchiefs
against moth, dust. Years later, I was surprised

by how they had kept
her smell. I had already learned to let go,

not expecting the grip of bergamot, of cloves.

Visit

Once a year the dead come back, not in dreams
or circled light, but as if they'd never left,
dwelling among their old things.

They pretend to remember who we are
while somehow knowing each of our names.
Grandma taps at the back window,

asks for coffee, weak. Mother serves it
on china I was sure she'd sold long ago.
Grandma says she can't believe Grandpa's still alive.

We agree. She never stays long. The cup
hardly makes a sound as she sets it in its saucer.
She's strong in a way she wasn't in life—

resolute, but not as stern.
We ask her what it's like.
She smiles a little sadly, and turns.

The Lady Eve

This time, Fonda dragged Stanwyck
straight to her cabin. How I lusted
for that kind of lust, for a kiss
on every landing.

At last weekend's wedding,
the bridesmaids moved in a cloud
of rip-off Chanel, their skirts open like hibiscus
inviting a bee's hairy graze.

I envied their cheek, their currency,
meant to buy a doctor, lawyer,
a house in the suburbs.
Stanwyck knew better

how to hook a man. She'd never tease her hair
to such heights, pay
for an extra cup size.
She needed only a heel to snag him

as it would a dead leaf. She knew disguise.
The bridesmaids have already forgotten
what their faces looked like,
stroking eyelashes curved into parentheses.

Persephone

The walls should be a pale blue, she decided,
in spite of the gray mist
that settled over everything.

The couch needed reupholstering
with something trendy:
paisley, say.

The seed at work in her body,
she wondered if his bed was better
than daffodils or sky.

She wished her mother could see
the ghostly curtains billowing,
the dark days by candlelight.

A Letter to Italy

You write that you've been ill. The garden
is fallow, sunflowers spitting seeds along the borders.
The factory is finally finished, you say,

and the neighbor's pasture will soon be a parking lot.
You're sleeping with a rosary, the new lemons
bending the branches, waiting. In Florida,

the sky is almost Mediterranean blue.
Even death is green. This is the land of adolescent palms,
so different from the muscled limbs

of olive trees. I remember the first night
you drove me to town. We sat in silence,
content to let the sun sink. You spent a year

teaching me to speak. Now we hardly exchange words,
though email and cell phones have invaded
Roman roads and stately Apennines.

Sometimes I think I see you at the supermarket,
a gray-haired woman with a silk scarf
and pumps, asking for help with the top shelf,

saying thank you without a smile.
You consider your lot not a burden, not light,
not without certain sacrifice.

The Things I Could Have Shown You

You drove through but decided not to stop
    after coming so far.
The sunlight was too calm to share,
    even had you wanted to see
my old house. Star-shaped pink blossoms
    wilted in the road,
as if thrown for newlyweds.
    Clouds spaced themselves
like a pointillist's dream.
    The porch, once muted green,
rolled up its sleeve to show a vein. Inside,
    you would have seen the dirty blinds
and other pleasantries: piles of overdue books,
    mismatched pillowcases. Instead,
you headed back to your world.
    Sometimes I wonder,
what do *I* want? It's easier,
    one of the noble truths, even,
to drown desire. It doesn't cost a thing, this love,
    until it costs everything.

The Far Side of the Mountain

Beneath the murk lay my fishing hat, somewhere
in the marina, his boat. I imagine the lake
as it once was: two low-lying towns, their graveyards,
the dead's peace disturbed for higher ground.

Mother never let us swim to the buoys,
so I drove back roads to the cliffs,
dove into a deeper green. Sugarloaf Mountain loomed,

the lone god of the lake. Now I see it
from the other side, a distant, pitiful shade.
I wonder if Eurydice, once back in Hades,
still hummed some song she'd heard Orpheus play.

Next Life

Just in case the roses wilt in an afternoon,
or prick us bloody, or give off a heavy stink,
in case the vase breaks or the water browns,
in case I fail to look at them before shutting
the door, regardless of their pitiful state,
in case I forget that there *were* flowers,
even though a few buds failed to open
or were pregnant with bugs, let me remember
the first long days after their arrival,
when I still believed in permanence
and that giving mattered more than gift.

Acknowledgments

Many thanks to the editors of the publications in which these poems first appeared, some in earlier versions.

"An Education" was selected for *Best New Poets 2018* (University of Virginia Press).

Cantos: "Ginkgo"
Cave Region Review: "Rapunzel," "Ghost Town"
Cellpoems: "Daffodil"
Coal Hill: "Chicken Farm"
Concho River Review: "Mercy"
Contemporary Verse 2: "Y2K"
Elder Mountain: "Summer, Greers Ferry Lake," "Mountain Air"
Empty House Press: "Diminuendo"
Epiphany: "At the Creek," "A week before she died"
Glassworks: "Flight"
Green Briar Review: "Childhood"
Impossible Task: "At the Jardin des Plantes," "The Little Mermaid Vacations in Florida," "Musée d'Orsay"
October Hill: "Leaving Rome"
Orson's Review: "The Far Side of the Mountain," "Cyclist with Two Bikes," "Home," "Visit"
Sixfold: "Emergence," "First Communion," "Milking," "Morrilton, Arkansas"
Slant: "The Lady Eve"
The Fem: "Epiphany"
The Timberline Review: "A Letter to Italy," "At the Coffee Shop," "A Monastery in Venice"
The Tishman Review: "Always a War"
Twyckenham Notes: "Still Life"
Summerset Review: "Airport," "Composition 912"

I would like to thank the earliest encouragers of my work, my parents and family, as well as my 5th grade teacher, Marilyn Seaton. Many thanks to the Gricia family, who hosted me for a year in Italy, and to Antonio Martino, Maria Scerrato, and Maria Grazia Mariani.

To my first writing professors, David Madden and Laura Mullen, as well as Sidney Wade, Michael Hofmann, and William Logan, I wish to express my gratitude for their instruction, example, and mentorship as well as their unwavering dedication to students and the craft of poetry. Many thanks to Sarah Grigg Rolph, Sam Grenrock, Ashley Tisdale, Brian Malatesta, Walter Smelt III, Adam Stengel, Victor Florence, and Gentris Jointe for their thoughtful suggestions and encouragement. I am grateful to the Sewanee Writers Conference as well as to Claudia Emerson and Robert Hass. Thank you to Jenn May, Shelby Lynne, Marla Grupe Williams, Sara Shumaker, Josh Markham, and Jennifer McCune. Finally, thank you to my confidant and steadfast partner in this life, Chuck.

About FutureCycle Press

FutureCycle Press is dedicated to publishing lasting English-language poetry in both print-on-demand and Kindle formats. Founded in 2007 by long-time independent editor/publishers and partners Diane Kistner and Robert S. King, the press was incorporated as a nonprofit in 2012. A number of our editors are distinguished poets and writers in their own right, and we have been actively involved in the small press movement going back to the early seventies.

Each year, we award the FutureCycle Poetry Book Prize and honorarium for the best original full-length volume of poetry we published that year. Introduced in 2013, proceeds from our Good Works projects are donated to charity. Our Selected Poems series highlights contemporary poets with a substantial body of work to their credit; with this series we strive to resurrect work that has had limited distribution and is now out of print.

We are dedicated to giving all of the authors we publish the care their work deserves, offering a catalog of the most diverse and distinguished work possible, and paying forward any earnings to fund more great books. All of our books are kept "alive" and available unless and until an author requests a title be taken out of print.

We've learned a few things about independent publishing over the years. We've also evolved a unique and resilient publishing model that allows us to focus mainly on vetting and preserving for posterity poetry collections of exceptional quality without becoming overwhelmed with bookkeeping and mailing, fundraising activities, or taxing editorial and production "bubbles." To find out more about what we are doing, come see us at futurecycle.org.

The FutureCycle Poetry Book Prize

All original, full-length poetry books published by FutureCycle Press in a given calendar year are considered for the annual FutureCycle Poetry Book Prize. This allows us to consider each submission on its own merits, outside of the context of a traditional contest. Too, the judges see the finished book, which will have benefitted from the beautiful book design and strong editorial gloss we are famous for.

The book ranked the best in judging is announced as the prize-winner in January of the subsequent year. There is no fixed monetary award; instead, the winning poet receives an honorarium of 20% of the total net royalties from all poetry books and chapbooks the press sold online in the year the winning book was published. The winner is also accorded the honor of being on the panel of judges for the next year's competition; all judges receive copies of the contending books to keep for their personal library.

Made in the USA
Coppell, TX
15 February 2022

73638042R00049